RISE

and

FLOAT

RISE

and

FLOAT

poems

BRIAN TIERNEY

Jake Adam York Prize | Selected by Randall Mann

MILKWEED EDITIONS

Published 2022 by Milkweed Editions
Printed in Canada
Cover design by Mary Austin Speaker
Cover art by Mary Austin Speaker
22 23 24 25 26   5 4 3 2 1
First Edition

Library of Congress Cataloging-in-Publication Data

Names: Tierney, Brian, 1985- author.
Title: Rise and float : poems / Brian Tierney.
Description: Minneapolis, Minnesota : Milkweed Editions, [2022] |
   Summary: "Chosen by Randall Mann as a winner of the Jake Adam
   York Prize, Brian Tierney's Rise and Float depicts the journey of a
   poet working-remarkably, miraculously-to make our most profound,
   private wounds visible on the page"-- Provided by publisher.
Identifiers: LCCN 2021030384 (print) | LCCN 2021030385 (ebook) |
   ISBN 9781571315199 (trade paperback) | ISBN 9781571317728 (ebook)
Subjects: LCGFT: Poetry.
Classification: LCC PS3620.I375 R57 2022 (print) | LCC PS3620.
   I375 (ebook) | DDC 811/.6--dc23
LC record available at https://lccn.loc.gov/2021030384
LC ebook record available at https://lccn.loc.gov/2021030385

Milkweed Editions is committed to ecological stewardship. We strive to align our book production practices with this principle, and to reduce the impact of our operations in the environment. We are a member of the Green Press Initiative, a nonprofit coalition of publishers, manufacturers, and authors working to protect the world's endangered forests and conserve natural resources. *Rise and Float* was printed on acid-free 100% postconsumer-waste paper by Friesens Corporation.

for my parents

Contents

one way with words is to tell
the lives of others
using the distance as a lens

and another way
is when there is no distance
so that water
is looking at water

W.S. Merwin

Wormhole

All winter, the house groaned as in a very great depth,
so that I often couldn't sleep. Then, one day, as if the inverse

of lightning, silence occurred, entrusted to the hour:
I became each minute, I became every direction at once

and fled from source and definite position, and returned
to my mother in plaid widow slippers, the blue flaking hallway

at the end of which she'd wrap gifts with the funny papers,
and I felt again the weight of her life shaping my fate—

When she paused, I paused. When she looked down I looked
as well, down, into the garden, at the material consequence

of a metaphysical truth: memorial flowers we'd planted,
then left. These rooms'll outlive you I had told her once

in spite, when I was younger, not young, while she hung
our shirts above and around a busted upright to dry in the sun

of a perfect angle, in which to watch was to surrender
metamorphic mystery, but, equally, fear. Having set aside

changes I could think of as tracks to be followed, future
possibilities, arguments of a speculative nature, the roads

with nobody on them, and with no one to remember anyone
who was, I walked into that garden. When I bent to them,

the impatiens soured and gave a small yelp; some of them
had names I could not take with me. Night fell. The treasure

I thought at the outset was wholeness, was not wholeness.
A passing car went white as the head of a match, and was gone.

Howard Johnson's

Four real pumpkins near the lobby door—

Their carved expressions sag
rural-sad, dissimilar, adjective adjective.

One eye droops. Melted angles. Smiles decaying.

Your cousin Rita's, after her stroke. Her oblique stroke
smiles, you remember:

She was embarrassed.

My face is not my own, looking down. Embarrassed.

There is a pen for workers out back labeled *staff*.
No one in sight
has left something behind. An ashtray
smokes then doesn't;

Friday night's lip gloss on a few white filters—

You approach. Across the highway, a sign
reads *What else is there? Isaiah 40:3.*

The glossy paint of the sign sort of shines.

rorschach #1

'The first mistake was to think
                    that Abraham had chosen
        to pause—'
            a splotch of ink—

        so I drop the topic
    like a box of books . . .

            He says 'Now tell me what you see'—

            Two tabbies
    judging a puddle
            at the end of our one-way, their tongues

        entering lightly
    as bugs;
            'Can you go
            deeper?'—   the grafted double oak

    always wigged with dead lichen
                        not moss
    Jess said, *not even Spanish moss*

    is moss: an Angel falling very slowly into a man, and a man

        ascending slowly
            the stairs, to a flat
                        black roof—

Greystone Park

derelict psychiatric hospital, New Jersey

I look down the corridor of shredded red paint and soft cream
messy-peeled, like wrist skin when a grater slips. *Water damage*

I say to Big Tim, with me on a dare here: an extension built
to relieve the Trenton mad-house seven train-stops south,

where you can buy cheap acid from a guy they call Lobotomy,
for the scar across his head. We take two small hits:

now scraps of trash greenly drift like unraveled petals
of water lettuce, in puddles, and I swear I hear breathing.

So which of these fuckers was hers? Meaning my great-aunt
Evelyn's, *her cell*, of course, *I don't know.* As I listen to Tim

kicking corroded metal instruments in a janitor's closet,
I hear it again: her silver spoon hitting the plate, going too

deep; her laugh as good as scream. Just a few stray anecdotes
she told us that breakfast—the leather tentacles squeaking

every flinch, gloves gripping a steering wheel winter,
how the shock machine in 1960 *felt all fog* as it breathed

behind her eyes, dissolved her spine, chlorpromazine in a glass
of water the first time—until each surrounding color had a

sound I imagine had no end but in the body. As in a drain.
Near the wall restraints, stains only butchers would've known

about. Rusting holes. Holes where holes are not supposed to be.

Eleven

a café

it must've been
The Dreaming Ant
Diner, given my age—

textured walls
painted eggplant

gold and white,

and the chime of white
cups so many lips

have touched,
the silver subtext

of the ordinary
spoons. My father's hands
are rain-

damp and smell
of corduroy

worn too long
in the sun
among the green

stems of beefsteak

tomatoes—

On the floor, the cast
shadow-grid

of the pastry rack
like a cage

neither open
nor closed, but nonetheless

dividing light

where it falls

Cottman Avenue House Party

Hour two, John's trying to take his shadow off.
On the neighbor's lawn, stray bottles arranged in green-
glass bouquets, I hear someone scream,
and the cock eyed towers of the poorly run junkyard
just behind Tim's groaning like cellos
unspooling in the wind; I recall the boy (when I was
a boy) who'd hopped its fence and was torn open
by its sentinel Dobermans, whose violence, we were told,
was *certainly atypical*. The owner, who shot them,
hung their tags from a mounted shuriken.
Somewhere above all that metal shit shifting I imagine
two beautiful teenagers are kissing. I recall pigeons,
televisions, fridges in there. Other winters, other
screams: my cousin Kristen's limp right hand
fanned open near the paint can in the suicide scene.

Teletherapy

The light of that

jet, overhead, is my mind I'm seeing so scintillant, unreachable.
I am never where my body is.
The first law of dreaming is what isn't here

isn't me; the second law is to show you what I see
is to show you how I feel: aluminum
siding the color of my skin
enwrapping the duplex where I lived, as a boy, by the ruins of a bridge

for what could not be united—
The message is frail.
When I check my phone

to remember I exist and I shake it and shake it I shake
myself, as if to clear the Etch A Sketch
of my face. If I'm dead inside

how would I know, how
would a bulb
check its own filament.

bulimia

On AM radio, a post-war hit—a courtship by sea—
that first time I emptied consciously. I focused on the xylophone
  to drown me out. In the tune, a boat
for two on one end was sinking
                                  through a modest raunch
meant to trick the children: *so many leaks, not ee-nough fingers,*
my sweet. When I put one in my mouth, I nearly touched the bell
  of my voice. I've done this for years, wanting
to be a love song
                                  a little less each week. An abstraction
too immense, like the Pacific's continent of trash
in crazy migration, accumulating summits I try to imagine
bear with them part of
                                  what I've released, unbelieving
the soul. What it is and what it becomes
  as it splashes into water
                                  makes a lovely sound, vanishing
shapes I can sometimes, almost, see myself in—an ant
hill; a dung heap; the beginnings of a moon
                                  there is no way to reach.

Ideation

Inside, the hole waits.

You avoid it. A day, an evening. You avoid it

by increments. Target on Wednesday. Another your brother
calling, cursing Mitch McConnell,

'that turkey fuckface,' and you laugh. Or you want to

but you don't laugh—

And you bed and you sleep and you sleep and you sleep . . .

And night. It is only the need
for reprieve

suspended. A treat sometimes

to hear the raccoons,
their leather hands

you count them. You count on the thought of their hands
the syllables of the opening lines of a friend's poem

that once saved your life
in a way—

You avoid it, the hole. In a way, you are already inside it.

You've stared into the hole

through the thought of the hole. The way a tunnel is
if you don't have headlights. It will not go all the way

to the other side. Not all at one time.

Time and Tide

The dream in which I see myself
born. The dream of mom
in her one good dress
kneeling to Thérèse, Saint of Lisieux,
The Little Flower who died of TB;
the irreality of her cheeks,
in that light, like sculpted Carrara marble
pears as hard as the tumor
in my father's neck, flat white in scans
he fanned out on a sewing table, to stare at
his fate; to know its contours—
I can trace for you the mountain,
later, we scattered with his
face, I can show you the puff of him
like magnesium smoke
stalled above an old photo flash-lamp,
but I can't play the sound of him
laughing before he was ill.
Is this what the book meant, observing
of mirrors their symmetry
is sinister, a subtractive delusion?
Is each keyhole smaller than the last?

Nothing Has Passed Between Us But Time

1.

To move through it quickly, on turnpike or park-
way, New Jersey is nearly beautiful in spring—
when vine helices and medusa weeds, week by week,
along these black routes, with devoted green logic,
scale the stanchions of premium billboards,
some of them lit severely from beneath. On one,
a bald child reclines beside a digital, glowing, cytotoxin
delivery machine, the kind which my father knew,

toward the end, as well as sick itself; the branch of
his right hand twitched in his skin like a filament,
I swear. He was magnificent that day. Not an hour's
drive from bodega x, in the city, where he met Mom
among veggies in stands, she says, when I ask, she
says the clerk said: *please don't bite the late tomatoes!*

2.

Please don't bite the late tomatoes, something like that,
yes, Mom says. Although she juggles *beefsteak* or *roma,*
maybe another. Finally conceding. That even the details die
by duration; that more than anything, setting survives
erasure. What she remembers: Saint something of something

next door. A fetid trash rain. Puddles full of neon worms.
There was twilight fog through which a ferry returned,
as from an afterlife—peopled by Italians still bowing

to the Madonna, some of them dressed utterly in black,
so that they appeared to her, in their huddle, cave-like.
She overheard her mother's mother's tongue, she thinks
dialetto lucano, which by then she had lost, same way she lost
the southern-Italian obsidian in her hair—*see?* she says,
and pulls taut her widow's peak, her gray-white roots.

3.

It was to show me her roots. 'That by this we may know
we confront the real.' If I paraphrase here, I do it, yes,
for fear. For the odd pleasure of after-hours sirens
in Paterson, how they advance in me a pedestrian love
that leaves a sort of stain, a faint spilled wine—
the steady sun dulling a curtain. A thought so tenuous
my father's chemo-swollen face breaks its surface,
calmly, like a turtle shell. But mom is not telling me

she is dying, she is telling me at length how she knew
a gent who kept, for luck, in his right breast pocket,
a Scotch-tape-salvaged three of clubs and a photo
from Naples. He showed her once the face it took
five minutes of stillness to capture: a bit starry,
like a European Jesus, is how she describes it.

18

4.

If I linger now. If I describe another photograph,
our Cardarella elders, two men in black slacks
smoking cigarillos by a silk mill just off Morris Canal,
it is because they have been waiting a long time
for the fall of my eyes, like animals glancing
out from a trap, their pupils black as the insides
of graves, of everything that is dying tonight,
and is like a fire choking on walls, and is not infinite;

the speckled fuzz at the end of the video-
tape I rewind again, again, a small resurrection:
Mom at thirty-six, in the hospital, un-kissing my father
as the first skin over my skull shrinks back
into the cradle of his hand, which, years later, turning
over the razor, I see is my hand, my disbelief.

＊

　　　　　　　　　　　　　　　＊

　＊

Episode

The corridor shines the same as day, any time of day.
In one neglected planter,
even the succulents are suffering

from stress. Read and read and touch
the message, always the same: having a body is a form
of courting peril—
Here, everything aches,
and, in this, the plot

becomes luminous, the sun faster
than rodents can eat some mornings, when I surface
to breathe, amazed,
in the air, after so long under—

the calmest hours always shorter,
my pace more measured.
I walk early to remember motion, possibility.

Not because I see it is the creek
a creek, but because I think it, one philosopher said,
and in thinking it
the place of the mind extends

to the sea. Essence, texture. In order to be one
with that thought he yelled
into the current: *I deny this reality!*

Hearses

A professor once wrote me that to write of fruit
or flowers or dreams, no matter how deftly,
is the lowest form of metaphor, after processions.
Years later, on the subject again, she that time
indicted horses as well, most especially wild ones,
even the word wild itself, *government-arrogated*,
legally defined, she meant, not by what the wild horses are,
as a species, but the context by which they roam
and where, and the manner in which
the land was theirs, she meant, was cheapened,
made public, an open space also owned—
plains I refuse to render, or re-populate,
having read only yesterday how after the sweeps,
which the Bureau of Land calls *mustanging*,
the colonial-Spanish feral descendants remain somehow
sentient during dismemberment, later sold;
I think the saw's sound, though an obsession of itself,
after a while, must be otherwise mundane,
no more than an idling truck full of Swedish Fish
my union friend drives from Hanover
east to Clifton and Passaic, then over the Passaic
River—its color, when rushing, a soiled denim
like my grandpa wore on the Morris Co. sewer crew
thirty-plus years, below the roads, breathing children's waste
from St. Mary's—and, eventually, the truck
of red treats arriving unseen at a 7-Eleven,
where a night clerk hands back
loose heads of presidents the customer trusts,

by combined weight, is the right change
for a ten or two fives, Lincoln and Roosevelt touching
inside a pocket, jingling as they pass,
adjacent to the door, a smell of cold roses
in a sad yellow bucket, similar to one I puked in one June,
several times, after waking from a nightmare
in which I was dying ignobly
in the back of a cab, a heart attack
on the Garden State Parkway, while a low-angled sun-
set beat the marshlands into flat metallic fields,
and beneath my hand on my galloping breast
I felt the angles of a matchbook, in my shirt pocket,
with its blue font reading *thank you! thank you! Please keep closed*,
as if against my heart lay the door to a stable.

Polyphagia

1.

—then my body said *I do*. And so indulgence came to me
    week after week, opening its hand like a late-nite diner
menu, impossible with options, page after page, so many

    words for *appetite*, so many preparations: the simplest
white plate, spent bones in a bramble, flies' eyes glistening
    on the gristle, it did not disgust me, the thought;

it only made me want more. How many ways can you fill
    a hole, I once asked a shrink, *it depends on the hole
I think*, and he scribbled something down, taking my order.

2.

                all that time me
thinking it was hunger, all that time, seeking some shadow,
    when it was a shadow seeking, going on within me,

wanting me to accede to its filling—the shape, that is,
    that traced my shape, which I fell through,
a skater through ice, and, after a while, my body like

a sponge swelling beneath the dark frigid water,
flooding what I'd mistaken for craving, each crook of it, each
    living, absorbent, coral pockmark calling and calling

with their little open mouths like baby robins . . . until,
    each time this happened, compulsion became one weight
sinking—like a fathometer testing
                                        limits, measuring
    emptiness, to see at what depth even god turns around.

3.

in the year it began I met a man I still think of—
    his cane staccato-tapping on a triangle park
path, chickening me with a stick of mint gum for a Marlboro

Gold cig, which I took, sort of reverently. He said *hazel
green*, into my eyes, *like my mom's*, then quoted Phoenicians
    and told me how she had died when he was young
from a different hunger,

some of which he took
with him, he smiled. And I thought of mom's uncle dead
    beneath a porch with a bourbon bottle and a head

of lettuce when a demo-crew found him.
Turns out rock bottom's not a problem, he said, *when you begin
                            without a bottom.*

To The Reasoning Of Eternal Voices, To The Waves That Have Kept Me From Reaching You—

In the photo negative, the sea is light. Holding it I think of your lung
and a spreading appears. Other winters—
The drip that by the bed filled the Folgers can with shit
every hour. How I read you the weather
and *Dharma Bums*. You said in time I'd understand Kerouac
was unworthy of the Buddha, then asked me to stop.
By then you'd lost your right front tooth,
which embarrassed me; you'd clear a corncob as if playing a flute,
whichever side of your mouth hurt less that day.
Which is maybe what you meant, that memory can be kind
of an accomplishment. The chaplain tracing a cross
of oil with his thumb on your forehead, and your eyes following
upward his hand, then holding, following,
holding. Like a kid who believes
he's watching a kite, when he's watching the breeze.

The Fly In The Bottle

Tim called to say Fentanyl Jen from Tacony-
Palmyra
jumped off the bridge

but lived? my god . . . And I said *god*,
but I meant I hope
our corpses keep

the trees awake forever—
And suddenly, at the thought, memory presents itself
like a yellow light
you gotta run through to beat

the cross-street traffic
near The Dreaming Ant Diner,
where in a cabbage-print dress and John Lennon shades
one summer,
in chemical distress,

Jen stabbed with her fork
her two sunny yolks,
saying *angels, my angels*, over and over, as if to coerce the eggs
back
into their caves,

as if to euthanize what might have been
her soul,
by which I mean her mind,

each time piercing what'd already deflated.

Tailpipe

Almost like a dream Tricia comes to me. I imagine the copper maw of the green garden hose, how it smelled of old keys and sun-tan lotion. I imagine the tailpipe and imagine her dozing and imagine her bullshit paperback novel, her reading material while waiting out oblivion—a book no one, according to legend, remembers the title of, though I suspect that's more suppression than amnesia. I imagine her voice which I have never heard and never will. In moments of weakness I sometimes imagine how she wears her hair in heaven, then recoil. I imagine the smell of oil in the garage and I imagine the engine, after a while, must've bucked and choked off and sounded pathetic, sputtering like a tractor, while she descended the poison. I imagine the silence of the rafters after she died, the absence above her asking to be filled. I imagine the bell alone in the field I once dreamed about after Dad was diagnosed. I imagine what mundane task sent grandpa to the garage that morning he found Tricia dead, curled up in a blanket with her thumb in that book. From the outside I imagine the garage less than ten feet away from the screened side door into the kitchen—the smell of Nana's rich gizzard gravy, which she would brown ceremoniously in cast-iron Depression-era pans during our summer visits. I imagine her kiss. I imagine setting out from that ranch house on Orange Street. How we'd sometimes walk the two blocks together to St. Mary's graveyard, where every family member is or will be buried. I imagine all the conifers swaying over Tricia there, and my father too, and my great-grandfather Paddy Joseph, ashamed of his hat trick of quasi-nervous breakdowns.

Tied Islands

Patio stones resembling the outlines of states—
Montana wet, post-rain, like an irritated eye.

When a bus goes by, my radio seltzers in and out
of blue-hour wavelengths. From the west, a stench

of sunset souping the reservoir. I consider this
as I step on Vermont, barefoot, the lower-left corner

where Bennington would be. And the stone warmer
than the air around it, where, in the real, maybe pine

trees, a field. The corpse of Frost
                            is under my heel.

Earth Is Not A Door

Curiosity tells us there are blue dunes
on Mars; that there was water, once, before us,
belonging to no one—
as though space exploration were a post-
colonial thought.

There are five U.S. flags left standing
on the moon, five dollars
each, stitched with nylon from Jersey, all of them
bleached into one color, now,
in the nation of nothingness. God says *I don't believe you.*
And Dr. Snaut goes on about how we don't want
other worlds, in the first film
Solaris; we just want

a mirror—which I take to mean we
cut down trees we press into reams on which we write
down our history of cutting
down the trees; or that space rocks crumble
then clump, like my Godmom Mar-ie
on the mantle, here, in front of me, even if I shake her
and make a stupid wish. The first of us
to occupy the Americas may not have
crossed Beringia Land Bridge, a new report
to believe

for now; just worm routes collapsing
behind us as we move. And I felt important

then, she said, my mother
that is, about her stint calibrating circuitry
chips with miniature instruments
for Apollo 11, when she needed money
for gas and college—

In her childhood room, what happened that one time
when we turned the two mirrors,
Sean and Constance and I,
what happened after we turned them
to face one another, in the sun, was
that the sun became an amplified burst
going down, coming in, the snow-whited walls
in that one perfect minute
I was standing inside
a star.

Bridge

Perhaps, it is cliché
that stops me, leaning over the railing
so many hands have touched,
my mind becoming the cloud shadows
two shades darker
than the Bay they drift on
shortly after noon,
as lunch crowds gather.
I tell myself I am not the lavender shit
of ordinary seagulls
on the pylon rocks below,
where spreading waves terminate, reborn as cannons
the students on a fieldtrip
just down from me
squawk at, feigning fear: boom spray
boom: the inevitable end-points of any arc
surprise them still. Standing here,
I understand. Even if
there is space, today, for a dream
of green islands in the distance between us,
my friends and me, I think
some of them
don't know me at all—

Preamble With Pilgrimage Inside

You're imagining *It* already
as something else: a citadel in a citadel
town. Or a town, maybe
your town, a city, maybe this city
street the journey will meet you at,
where no one hails a cab
they won't fight for
in the rain, the parking-lot puddles
as large as small ponds
mirrored streetlights, late night, squirm upon
the surface of, like clusters of grubs
that, struggling, seem to sink
and disappear—into indifferent darkness
a kind of throne is born from.
Or maybe location doesn't matter
in the century of the bomb.
Maybe you'll go on as a cell goes
on, a hundred cells within
a cell, and each cell a moment
awaiting a saint to bring you photosynthesis.
You want to call this *eternity*
on earth, the sacred site you've imagined
throwing your many prayers at,
your stored pouch of pennies
oxidized by water and light and maybe
you're right: It's a mountain
to climb, It's a cloud-castle umber
with sun, you thought you saw *It* in a water-

color cross at the watercolor end
of a watercolor trail
a crowd flowed up, toward
where Golgotha was
bare and unbeautiful, Christ a bird
just about to fly; a cheap reproduction
you could hold in your hand,
as scale would have it. *Thou art small
in thy life*, can you not see?

Fixing A Hole

One uncle was shocked the year Korea ended. My great-aunt was shocked. Great-grandfather shocked. His older sister, Evelyn, shocked in Greystone Park, while in a mostly paper room, where nothing had an edge, Woody Guthrie twisted pilfered twine into strings, using two to braid a tight, single E. I thought of his hands all the time, said X. I am only telling you what I couldn't have seen. Gripping the line that goes straight to the machine, to the temple, to Cousin Kristen and another I can't name. One great-aunt from Yonkers put it this way: a sort of snow drifting nighttime trenches. My brother tells me: I keep having this nightmare, a migraine light beating off a plate, you know—a bright wall of water, sometimes crystalline, obscuring a cave.

To The Felled Cherry Plum

And suddenly you said *names, I want*
names—

And so I carved 'Bitondo'

on your elephant trunk
soured by aphids, terminal gray

but elegant still.
Like Lou Reed's *Berlin*.

That last evening
I touched you uncut

I also dreamed I was next to you and the memory
of your wholeness remained
somehow

suggested
by dismemberment: pieces

so enormous and fresh,
they almost made a sound

with their shining
hardened sap

leaching out. Among your pile of limbs
the last of your fruits
like split-lips

a bee had already claimed
with its one barb

showing—and it would kill itself

to protect itself.

Breakdown

They raze swiftly each interstate mystery.
The haunted house.
The Astrolabe. The silent calliope, emptied of air, ornate
as a head-of-state's coffin

on wheels, its gold-
painted spokes, its faux-ivory panels
as chipped and streaked

as my mother's teeth were then—
which, even in memory, she can't afford
to fix. This is in lieu of

what I really want to say.

In an hour, the children we were here
will sleep, forgetting
their bodies, forgetting

umbilical air gun stalls, the feel of
the handles and the reigns
of the horses speared through on poles, for travel
unmounted lying side by side

like a Civil War still life together in the fennel
as tall as a person, taller even

than parents among the patrons, with their paper cones

of sugar as they leave, sweeter
than soda, sweeter even
than Matthew, the pear taste on his lips

I savor any time I eat
a Waldorf salad, suddenly younger and
with him again, re-watching

the caravan prep its procession
to some next destination: de-christened hearses
and escort vans, Econo-Trailers
and towing booths

and tosser-stands, from which
any one of us could buy
brass rings to throw through

a cardboard circle of a Bengal's mouth, and beyond
its black drape, its rough crepe
synth-linen mix, with its fabric stars
affixed comically

to the drape—behind which, if you dared
peel it for a peek between shifts,

while the vendor on break
would be rolling a joint with his boo-boo
stash, behind all that you'd see

each dollar-twenty fate, each zil
where it fell unseen

behind the drape, into a daisy-print bucket
filled with them they'd leave

til near end, the carnies, or whatever we call them
now, needing two of them
to lift it, and sometimes more.

All Stars Are Lights, Not All Lights Are Stars

What's next, I see it. Balancing there like a melon

on the point of a stick distracting bears, soon, no one will remember,

save fabulist painters in their plein-air

yellow gas masks. I see a nest of pupils and someone

says *we.* I'm trying, these days, to believe again

in people. Uncle "King" James, in his baker's apron, blotto

in Philly, asking each wallet *will you listen, please,* and I said *yes, I will*

listen—and stared into his eyes. As if looking through a fence

at where a building had been.

                         I see heaven

is not a place, it's a concept for pain, a pattern of snow

on municipal metal stairs I'm ascending now,

leading nowhere I know but a good place to lie

down. And hope I roll off. And make a seraph where I fall.

Judas

You turn away?
No one for miles reveres angels anymore.
Look: the chair is just a chair.
It's just milkweed at the window, the Red Roof
sign hissing awful things while you dream
small birds are rebuilding a cheek
in the image of a nest. Believe me I know
how deep god can go—as though it mattered
to the dirt. Which is maybe where the story leads.
Someone had to bleed first.
The ten-carat cross your father wore
on his lapel through two wars
is just an emblem that bore a fate
that is a symbol of a symbol. See?—
how the subject quakes? That too's a noose.
You just try and you'll see, Mr. I-
wore-a-scapular-once: there's no one
kind of love that complicates
the dark. December, none of it, means nothing
and nobody, and nobody
    sleeps. Jesus was a liar.

Whatever Won't Rise Becomes the Night

In the mouth of Poquessing, cuticles of bread drift toward me.
One boy, on the other bank, pursuing his sibling shouts *bang! bang!*
His brother hangs from a tire swing
and the sound of the rope with Kristen on one end,
in college, reaches deeper into me
than any elegy could go. The end of winter lingering
in the sewage, which is to say I left her there—
where the reign of rage has only begun.
Her blue robe shed to the floor like the queenly pelt
of a great blue bear.

Migraine

It starts at the end: the lights of cars
distorted to a burst, for a second

like asterisks extravagant and huge,
arguments shining. In the exhausted fog

over Mars, PA, then Punxsutawney
and New Stanton, on The Turnpike

in the rain, cars sweep and continue to
pass, en route to Erie, or Breezewood,

where their lives have been decided
by now. Pulled over, outside Somerset,

in my eyes all things look scintillant,
each thought a texture; otherworldy

filaments hang above a broke-open rodent
its head a hammered pomegranate—

useless, even to birds. It hurts to look at,
like blood coughed up in a bathtub.

My old man, the story goes, right before
he died, shouldered the Windstar

to phone her, me, anyone on his way
somewhere east of Poquessing, a faint red

fingertip print smeared on the dash,
as though someone had crushed a clover mite.

Anthropocene

1.

The short night—
at the foot of a stop sign standing
   red   water.

2.

Middling scotch I pair with pears, vanilla-bean ice cream.
Ants march toward clear liquid
poison by the door. On the covered porch,
I smell warm trash bags;
the chain of a flag keeps hitting its pole.

3.

Morning neighbor!
And their one dog, brindled, barks five times
   at the yellow train.

4.

Rain midday;

Across the patio, worms crawling
bunker to bunker;
they seem to be injured.

5.

On light rail to Berkeley I see things explain themselves:
a turning lane, its worn white arrow;
two hedges grown into one green gate.

Finding a yard sale, late in the day, I choose the pewter
ice-cream scoop; I scrutinize a picture
frame; I hold a stranger's elders in my hand.

6.

John is that you I keep hearing
voices   I say
            as I wake,

                    my wife tells me.

7.

I can't see the foot-hills, shrouded—
Nor Grizzly Peak, partially finished,
or partially erased. Who can say.

8.

Another dream:

a nervy me,
no larger than a chickaree,
paused on a branch,
    looks me, once, in the eye,
            then shits.

9.

Cigarette on the porch:

Wolf moon, but the usual fog; nothing seen
but the backdoor light, a gauzy beam,
a slanted rhombus portal on the lawn.
Avoiding it, a neighbor's mottled cat moves on.

10.

Our teeth are black,
and some of us smiling, others
    straining to—

I remember the bell of the basement phone ringing;

    on the table, four down cards
and a court card I think it was
    hearts; the face of a king.

11.

How slow
    its journey, over the Jersey-
shaped patio stone, the snail's:
                still quicker than rot.

12.

A U.S. flag drips after two days' rain, *heavy*
at times : the public trails I think now are wider.

13.

fortune cookie:

smile tomorrow
will present with you a chance—
And when I read it aloud
her slow chuckle rises through the quiet
in my chest,
like horsehair under water.

14.

In the house, wine glasses touch and make a bell.
The grass is wet I am walking on
hell's ceiling, as Buson puts it.
I think of all my dead, my cousin ten years.
As for the hose I mistake for a snake—
wearing long pants, I still avoid it.

15.

I saw your face for at least ten seconds—
What did it matter, my dreaming, after all?

16.

And now the crane swings its load arm,
and my radio gurgles low then straightens,
and my radio says a new bomb is born

As I come upon a shortcut I shake
the bent, overgrown, municipal fence

someone's snipped a passage through,
for which I make myself small,
but still can't walk through.

You're the One I Wanna Watch
the Last Ships Go Down With

for Jess

Dr. Redacted will tell me not to tell you
this, *like* this,
in a poem: how it's all right, love, that we don't love
living. Even actors don't
exactly love the spotlight they move through,
as your sister, the actor,
has told us; they just need to be lit
for narrative motion
to have meaning. As such it is,
with artifice, and embarrassment,
that I move through fear
to you, tonight, where I had dreams,
a short nap ago, about lines
of poetry I struck through
with everyday blues, month after
month, in the dream
after dream; an attempt
I guess to forget, if I could: defeat
sometimes is defeat
without purpose. The news at least tells me that
much. I know now,
in fact, we don't have to be brave,
not to survive a night
like any we've looked on
together, seeing blue-tinted snow
once in a K-mart

parking lot's giant, two-headed lamp—
and my father hooked up,
up the street, with no chance
of waking—as many years ago now
as how much longer I've lived
with you than without.
Forgive me, again, that I write you an elegy
where a love poem should be.

Notes

"All Stars Are Lights, Not All Lights Are Stars": The title is taken from Charles Wright's *Black Zodiac*.

"Anthropocene": This poem is inspired by Yosa Buson's "Spring Wind On The Riverbank Kema," as translated by Robert Hass. The phrase "the short night" is a nod to Buson, whose uses it in several haikus as a seasonal signal; "I am walking on / hell's ceiling" is from a famous Buson haiku, a derivation of Hass's translation.

"Bridge": The phrase *a dream of green islands* is borrowed from Eugenio Montale, as translated from the Italian by William Arrowsmith.

"Earth Is Not A Door": The title is borrowed and tweaked from James Wright.

"Episode": The phrase *I deny this reality!* is borrowed from an episode of *Doctor Who*.

"Ideation" is inspired by and dedicated to William Brewer.

"Judas": The line *see how the subject quakes?* is borrowed from *King Lear*, Act IV, scene 6.

"Nothing Has Passed Between Us But Time": The title is borrowed from Robert Lowell.

"To The Reasoning Of Eternal Voices . . . ": The title is borrowed from "To The Harbormaster" by Frank O'Hara; the line "memory can be / kind of an accomplishment" is borrowed from William Carlos Williams.

"Wormhole": The phrase "these rooms'll outlive you" is refracted from George Oppen; the phrase "names I could not take with me" is inspired by Larry Levis

"You're the One I Wanna Watch the Last Ships Go Down With": The title is borrowed from Father John Misty.

Acknowledgments

My sincere gratitude to the editors of the following publications, in which these poems and versions of these poems first appeared, sometimes with different titles:

Adroit Journal, AGNI, Copper Nickel, FIELD, Gettysburg Review, Jewish Currents, New England Review, Paris Review, Poetry Northwest, The Literary Review, Southern Indiana Review, Washington Square Review, West Branch, Yale Review. "All Stars Are Lights, Not All Lights Are Stars" was originally published on the Poetry Society of America's website (awarded the George Bogin Memorial Award), and "Polyphagia" originally appeared in *Frontier Poetry*, which awarded the poem second place for its 2018 Industry Prize.

Many thanks to the Stegner Program at Stanford University, and all my workshop mates and teachers and friends therein, all of whom guided me in so many ways, including Eavan Boland, Ken Fields, Simone DiPiero, Edgar Kunz, Casey Thayer, Margaret Ross, Corey Van Landingham, Rosalie Moffet, Solmaz Sharif, Ari Banias, Essy Stone, Matt Moser Miller, Grady Chambers, Laura Romeyn, and Michael Shewmaker. Thanks, as well, to Jimmie Cumbie, Sarah Phillips, Tony Tallon, and the astronaut cowboy, Barrett Warner, for their friendship and support in difficult times.

Endless gratitude to my teachers and mentors: Louise Glück, Tracy K. Smith, Timothy Liu, Major Jackson, April Bernard, Mark Wunderlich, Linda and Tom Kinnahan, and John Fried.

To Tim Schmid: it all started with songs; thank you, brother.

I want to thank Justin Kishbaugh, who early on showed me a life in poetry is a worthy life.

Special thanks to the incomparable dream-maker Randall Mann for believing in the work, and to William Brewer and Noah Warren, whose keen insights incalculably improved this book and whose friendship has always helped me keep the fire lit.

Thank you to my family—Sean, Audrey, Nancy, Brad, Sam, Dustin— for the love and support, and most especially Louisa, my mother, who gave me the heart and mind to be a poet.

To my love and partner in life, Jess Eagle: You're in everything I write; the two of us, through it all.

Jess Eagle

Brian Tierney's poetry and prose have appeared in *Paris Review, AGNI, Kenyon Review, NER, Adroit Journal*, and others. A graduate of the Bennington Writing Seminars, he is a former Wallace Stegner Fellow in poetry at Stanford and winner of the Poetry Society of America's 2018 George Bogin Memorial Award. He grew up in Philadelphia and currently lives in Oakland, where he teaches poetry at The Writing Salon.

The Jake Adam York Prize for a first or second collection of poems was established in 2016 to honor the name and legacy of Jake Adam York (1972-2012). York was the founder of *Copper Nickel*, a nationally distributed literary journal at the University of Colorado Denver. His work as a poet and scholar explored memory and social history, and particularly the Civil Rights Movement.

The judge for the 2020-21 Jake Adam York Prize was Randall Mann.

milkweed
editions

Founded as a nonprofit organization in 1980, Milkweed Editions is an independent publisher. Our mission is to identify, nurture and publish transformative literature, and build an engaged community around it.

Milkweed Editions is based in Bdé Óta Othúŋwe (Minneapolis) within Mní Sota Makhóčhe, the traditional homeland of the Dakhóta people. Residing here since time immemorial, Dakhóta people still call Mní Sota Makhóčhe home, with four federally recognized Dakhóta nations and many more Dakhóta people residing in what is now the state of Minnesota. Due to continued legacies of colonization, genocide, and forced removal, generations of Dakhóta people remain disenfranchised from their traditional homeland. Presently, Mní Sota Makhóčhe has become a refuge and home for many Indigenous nations and peoples, including seven federally recognized Ojibwe nations. We humbly encourage our readers to reflect upon the historical legacies held in the lands they occupy.

milkweed.org

Milkweed Editions, an independent nonprofit publisher, gratefully acknowledges sustaining support from our Board of Directors; the Alan B. Slifka Foundation and its president, Riva Ariella Ritvo-Slifka; the Amazon Literary Partnership; the Ballard Spahr Foundation; *Copper Nickel*; the McKnight Foundation; the National Endowment for the Arts; the National Poetry Series; the Target Foundation; and other generous contributions from foundations, corporations, and individuals. Also, this activity is made possible by the voters of Minnesota through a Minnesota State Arts Board Operating Support grant, thanks to a legislative appropriation from the arts and cultural heritage fund. For a full listing of Milkweed Editions supporters, please visit milkweed.org.

Interior design by Tijqua Daiker and Mary Austin Speaker
Typeset in Vendetta

Vendetta was designed in 1999 by John Downer. Inspired by
the class of types known as Venetian Old Style, Downer designed
Vendetta while considering the relationship between lowercase
letters and capital letters in terms of classical
ideals and geometric porportions. Vendetta
can be characterized by its synthesis
of ideas, old and new.